MINIMUS

Starting out in Latin

Barbara Bell

Joint Association of Classical Teachers

Illustrations by **Helen Forte**

CAMBRIDGE
UNIVERSITY PRESS

CAMBRIDGE UNIVERSITY PRESS
Cambridge, New York, Melbourne, Madrid, Cape Town, Singapore,
São Paulo, Delhi, Dubai, Tokyo, Mexico City

Cambridge University Press
The Edinburgh Building, Cambridge CB2 8RU, UK

www.cambridge.org
Information on this title: www.cambridge.org/9780521659604

First published 1999
18th printing 2010

Printed in the United Kingdom by Latimer Trend

Designed by Angela Ashton

A catalogue record for this publication is available from the British Library

ISBN 978-0-521-65960-4 Paperback

ACKNOWLEDGEMENTS

Thanks are due to the following for permission to reproduce photographs:

p. 5, p. 23 *t*, *b*, p. 30, p. 55 *t*, © The British Museum; p.6, p. 13, p. 23 *c*, p. 44 *l*, p. 60 *r*,
Vindolanda Trust; p. 24, Corbridge Museum and English Heritage Photographic Library; p. 44 *r*,
p. 51, p. 60 *l*, courtesy of the Museum of London; p. 55 *b*, p. 70, Museum of Antiquities of the
University and Society of Antiquaries of Newcastle upon Tyne.

Every effort has been made to locate copyright holders for all material in this book. The publisher
would be happy to hear from anyone whose copyright has been unwittingly infringed.

Contents

Introduction

Nearly 2,000 years ago, Britain was conquered by the Romans, and the Britons became part of the huge Roman Empire. The Roman family that you are going to read about lived in the north of Britain, at a place called Vindolanda.

Look at this map of Roman Britain, and find Vindolanda. It is close to Hadrian's Wall.

About 75 years after the Romans arrived, the Roman Emperor Hadrian came to Britain and ordered his soldiers to build a great wall. The soldiers then had to patrol the wall. It is known as Hadrian's Wall, and you can still see parts of it today. It stretches across the north of Britain from east to west, and passes near to Vindolanda.

That's where I live!

Meet the family

Who are you?

 WORDS TO HELP

quis es? Who are you? (*said to one person*)
quī estis? Who are you? (*said to more than one person*)
māter mother
pater father   **īnfāns** little child
fīlia daughter   **servī** slaves
fīlius son   **Vindolandae** at Vindolanda

In the picture story you met the Latin words which mean "I am",
"you are", and "we are". Here they are again:

sum   I am
es   you are (*when "you" is one person*)
sumus   we are
estis   you are (*when "you" is more than one person*)

GRASP THE GRAMMAR

Have another look at the picture story, where you met Flavius and his family. In the Latin sentences you met a number of **nouns**. A noun is a naming word, like **mūs** (a mouse), **fēlēs** (a cat), **māter** (a mother), and the name **Flāvia**.

1 Using the Latin word for "I am", introduce yourself to a partner. Try to make your name sound like a Latin name. Add **-us** to your name if you are a boy and add **-a** if you are a girl. So Marc will be **Marcus**, and Helen will be **Helena**.

2 Ask your partner his or her name by asking the Latin question which means "Who are you?"

N.B. (This is short for a Latin phrase – **nōtā bene** – which means "note well".) The men and boys have names ending in **-us,** for example Flavius and Corinthus. The women and girls have names ending in **-a,** for example Flavia and Lepidina.

ROMAN REPORT

Flavius, the father of our family, is in charge of the Roman fort at Vindolanda. He and his family lived there in about AD 97–102.

When you come across dates in history, it is important to check whether they refer to a time BC (before Christ) or AD (after Christ). AD is short for another Latin phrase, **annō dominī**, which means "in the year of our Lord".

55 and 54 BC — Julius Caesar, a Roman general, brings his army to Britain but doesn't stay long.

0 — Christ is born in the Roman province of Palestine.

AD 43 — The Roman Emperor Claudius invades Britain and conquers it.

AD 66 — Celtic queen Boudicca rebels, burns London, but is defeated.

AD 100 — Flavius and his family live at Vindolanda.

AD 122 — The Emperor Hadrian builds a wall across northern Britain.

The birthday party

One day, Lepidina receives an exciting letter from her friend Claudia, who lives in another Roman fort.

cārissima Lepīdina,
iii īdūs Septembrēs, venī ad diem nātālem meum.
valē, soror, anima mea.
Claudia

 WORDS TO HELP

cārissima dearest
iii īdūs the eleventh
diem nātālem birthday

soror sister
anima soul

This photograph shows the actual birthday invitation, found at Vindolanda.

Lepidina arrives at the party.

WORDS TO HELP

salvē! hello (*to one person*)
salvēte! hello (*to more than one person*)
omnēs everyone
exspectātissimus very welcome
dōnum a present
tibi for you
habeō I have
fēlīx diēs tibi sit! Happy Birthday!
  (*May you have a happy day!*)

grātiās tibi agō I thank you
quam pulcher how beautiful
sed but
quid? what?
fāmōsa famous
sedēte! sit down!
ōlim once upon a time

Claudia entertains her guests by telling them the Greek myth.

PERSEUS AND MEDUSA

Long ago, in Greece, lived a girl called Medusa, who was beautiful but proud and cruel. She made the gods angry, so to punish her they turned her into a monster. Her lovely hair came alive, a tangled nest of hissing snakes. Her face became so ugly that anyone who looked straight at her turned to stone. Full of hate and bitterness, she spread terror through the land. Many men tried to defeat the monstrous Medusa, but all failed.

Far away, a young hero called Perseus swore to kill Medusa, and set out bravely on this almost impossible quest. Luckily, the gods helped him. They lent him winged sandals, a magic sickle and a shiny bronze shield. Perseus flew for days until he reached Medusa's lair. He found her fast asleep and snoring, surrounded by stone statues of terrified men. Looking only at Medusa's reflection in his shield, Perseus cut off her head and flew home.

> Remember! A noun is a naming word for a person, a place or a thing.

WORDS TO REMEMBER

sum I am	**estis** you are **	**salvēte** hello**
es you are*	**sedēte!** sit!**	**omnēs** everyone
sumus we are	**salvē** hello*	**quis?** who?
		quid? what?

* you (*one person*)   ** you (*more than one person*)

Food, glorious food!

The Governor is coming!

Flavius and Lepidina have received a letter telling them that Marcellus, the Governor of Britain, is coming to see them at Vindolanda. The family prepares for this important visitor.

1. ēheu! vīlla sordida est.

2. ēheu! hortus squālidus est.

3. ēheu! tunica nōn pulchra est.

4. Lepidina tells Candidus to clean the house and tidy up the garden. Then he must cook a magnificent dinner. Corinthus must order a special dinner service from **Londinium***, and he must buy the best wine.
   *Can you guess what this city is called today?

5. ēheu! servī fessī sumus.

6. euge! Marcellus mīles optimus est!

7. euge! cibus optimus erit!

8. euge! Minimus obēsus erit!

WORDS TO HELP

ēheu! oh dear! **hortus** garden **fessī** tired
vīlla house **squālidus** messy **euge!** hooray!
sordida dirty **tunica** dress **mīles** soldier

> Why do you think that Lepidina, Flavius and Flavia are worried about the Governor's visit? Remember that Marcellus is in charge of the whole of Britain.
>
> Why are Candidus and Corinthus not pleased about it?
>
> Why is Iulius excited about Marcellus's visit?
>
> And why is the visit good for Minimus? And Vibrissa?

GRASP THE GRAMMAR

In chapter 1 you learnt that a **noun** is a naming word for a person, a place or a thing. Our writing becomes much more interesting when we *describe* the nouns. The words we use to describe nouns are called **adjectives**.

The word "desk" is a **noun**, because it's a thing. You might describe it with an **adjective** like "new", "old", "wooden", "scratched", "big" or "rectangular".

Nouns which end in **-a** are called feminine nouns (like **vīlla**, **tunica** and the name, **Flāvia**). Nouns which end in **-us** are called masculine nouns (like **hortus** and the name, **Flāvius**).

1 Have another look at the picture story.
Lepidina describes the house as "dirty": **vīlla sordida.**
Flavius describes the garden as "messy": **hortus squālidus.**

> Can you see that the ending of the adjective matches the ending of the noun?

Look at picture 3. Which Latin **noun** means "dress"? Which **adjective** describes it? Are these words masculine or feminine?

2 These sentences describe animals. The animal names are nouns. Each sentence has one noun and one adjective. Can you translate them into English?

| a vēspa parva est. | b bālaena maxima est. | c cunīculus improbus est. |
| d delphīnus benignus est. | e equus māgnus est. | f porcus sordidus est. |

Every sentence also contains the important word **est**. Do you remember what it means?

 WORDS TO HELP

vēspa wasp	**cunīculus** rabbit	**benignus** friendly
parva small	**improbus** naughty	**māgnus** big
bālaena whale	**delphīnus** dolphin	**porcus** pig
maxima very big		

 How did you do? If you got most of them right, you are **callidissima** (if you're a girl) or **callidissimus** (if you're a boy). It means "very clever"!

3 Describe yourself to a partner. Remember, the adjective you use must have the right ending: **-us** for a boy, and **-a** for a girl. You'll need the Latin word **sum** ("I am") too. Now describe your partner, or perhaps your teacher. Use the word **est** for "he is" or "she is".

 WORDS TO HELP

bonus/bona good	**māgnus/māgna** big
callidus/callida clever	**minimus/minima** very small
fōrmōsus/fōrmōsa beautiful	**optimus/optima** very good
ignāvus/ignāva lazy	**parvus/parva** small
improbus/improba naughty	**strēnuus/strēnua** energetic

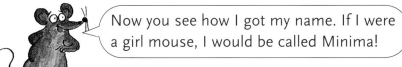 Now you see how I got my name. If I were a girl mouse, I would be called Minima!

LATIN ROOTS

In these sentences, the words which are underlined all come from Latin. Some of them may be new to you. Write down the Latin word that each of the underlined English words comes from. Then write down what you think these words mean. (To help answer the questions, look back at the words on page 10.)

1 What animal does <u>pork</u> come from?

2 What would an <u>equestrian</u> statue look like?

3 If you scored the <u>maximum</u> points in a test, would you be happy?

4 If you put <u>minimal</u> effort into your work, would your teacher be pleased with you?

ROMAN REPORT

Roman food

Candidus is planning a special dinner for the Governor's visit. The Romans did not eat much for breakfast or lunch, but they ate a big meal which began late in the afternoon. This was known as the **cēna**. A wealthy Roman would provide his guests with an impressive meal, and might offer poetry, singing or even an acrobatic display to amuse them as they ate. Even at Vindolanda, at the far end of the Roman Empire, Flavius could give his guests a wonderful dinner, with special wine and food such as oysters and venison.

The Romans ate many of the foods that we enjoy today: chicken, pork, fish, and lots of vegetables and fruit. They also ate things which we would think strange – or even disgusting – like stuffed dormice! Roman cooks made a rich fish sauce called **liquāmen** which they used in many recipes. Guests enjoyed plenty of wine at the **cēna**, though it was mixed with water.

The soldiers under Flavius's command would have eaten simpler foods like bread, vegetables, bacon and ham. At Vindolanda they also drank beer.

Dinner for the Governor

Everyone is ready for the special dinner. The place of honour is reserved for Marcellus, the Governor. Candidus and Corinthus have brought in the food. But where is Rufus?

vir optime sir
cāseus cheese
surge! get up!
nunc now
nōlī tangere don't touch
omnēs silent everyone is silent

redī go back
cubiculum bedroom
nōlī lacrimāre don't cry
scīlicet of course
rīdent smiles
praecipuē especially

This photo shows
some pottery found
at Vindolanda

Marcellus tells the story of another boy who, like Rufus, didn't listen to his father!

DAEDALUS AND ICARUS

Minos, King of Crete, asked Daedalus, a famous designer and inventor, to build a maze for him. However, as soon as the maze was finished, the king became angry with Daedalus and locked him and his son Icarus away in a tower on his island.

They could not escape by land or sea. Daedalus was determined to get away, and he used his skills to make wings for himself and for Icarus by joining feathers together with thread and wax. When Daedalus attached the wings to their arms, they were able to fly up into the sky.

"Fly close by me," Daedalus warned his son. "If you fly too high, the sun will melt the wax. If you dive too low, the sea will make the feathers wet."

Daedalus flew safely to Sicily, but Icarus disobeyed his father's instructions. He flew too close to the sun. The wax melted, the feathers fell off, and the boy plunged into the sea.

Remember that adjectives are describing words which tell us more about nouns.

WORDS TO REMEMBER

servī slaves	**bonus/bona** good
mīles soldier	**optimus/optima** very good
cibus food	**ēheu!** oh dear!
vīlla house	**euge!** hooray!
parvus/parva small	**sedē** sit
improbus/improba naughty	**nōlī lacrimāre** don't cry

What are you doing?

Everyone is busy in Flavius's household.

WORDS TO HELP

facis you are doing
scrībō I am writing
scrībit he is writing
spectat he is watching
pūrgō I am cleaning
pūrgat he is cleaning
legō I am reading
legit he is reading

verrō I am sweeping
subitō suddenly
ancilla slave girl
intrat she is entering
nova new
nunc now
labōrant they are working
rīdent they are smiling

GRASP THE GRAMMAR

In the picture story, each of the people is doing something. The words we use to talk about actions are called **verbs**, for example: Corinthus **is writing** and Candidus **is cleaning**. What is Rufus doing?

1 Have another look at the picture story. Find the Latin words which tell you what the characters are doing. These words – the **verbs** – come at the end of each sentence. Write down the **verbs** in Latin and then write the English meaning next to each one, for example: **scrībit** he is writing.

I want you to remember that if a verb ends in **-t**, then *he* or *she* is doing that action.

2 Now look back at the picture story to see who is doing the action when the verb ends in **-ō** or **-nt**.

In Latin you don't need to use a separate word for "I" or "he" or "they". **The ending of the verb tells us who is doing the action.**

3 Write down these Latin verbs. Circle the ending which tells you **who** is doing the action. Then write down the English meaning of the word, making it clear who is doing the action.

    a scrībit   **e** sprecta**nt**
    b spectat   **f** facis
    c spectō   **g** scrību**nt**
    d scrībō   **h** scrībi**s**

ROMAN REPORT

Who are the slaves?

Corinthus is a slave from Greece. He has lived with Flavius and Lepidina for many years. He is very clever, and can read and write well. He can speak Greek as well as Latin.

Candidus has always lived in Britain. When the family arrived at Vindolanda, they bought him as a slave. He speaks a Celtic language, and is learning to speak Latin. He is a good cook, so he is a valuable slave, and he is treated kindly by Flavius and Lepidina.

Pandora is a new slave girl. Lepidina is pleased to have her, because she is a very good hairdresser.

Slaves were not paid for their work but were given a little pocket-money. Sometimes slaves saved their money to buy their freedom. If they had been good and faithful slaves, they might be given their freedom in their master's will. Or he might invite them to join him at the evening dinner. This was a sign that they were now free.

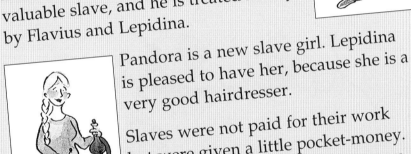

Look carefully at the pictures of Corinthus and Candidus. Is there anything about their clothes which suggests where they come from or what kind of slaves they are?

Pandora settles in

The two slaves are having a competition. They both want to impress Pandora.

WORDS TO HELP

quod because   **coquis** you cook
minimē! no   **validus** strong
legis you read   **semper** always

PANDORA'S BOX

The Greeks told this story to explain how trouble came
into the world. When the world was young, and men
were new and perfect, Jupiter, King of the gods,
became afraid. What if these humans tried to take over
from him? He studied them carefully, and then came up
with a plan. Jupiter asked Vulcan, god of craft and skill, to
make a woman out of clay. The gods then gave her gifts of
beauty, kindness and grace. Jupiter brought her to life and
named her Pandora. He led her to Earth, to a house where a man
called Epimetheus lived. Epimetheus was a good but simple man
and Jupiter gave him Pandora as his bride. He also gave them a
box, with strict instructions not
to open it.

Pandora was happy with
her husband but she kept
thinking about the
strange box. Why
shouldn't she open it?
She grew more and more
curious, just as Jupiter had intended. Eventually, she couldn't
stand it any longer. She took out the box and opened the lid.
Immediately a cloud of flying, stinging creatures filled the air.
They were all the troubles of humanity – disease, hate, anger, old
age and many more. Pandora tried to shut the lid but it was too
late. Only one thing was left, shining in a corner of the box. It
was Hope. Humans would never trouble Jupiter now, with so
many troubles of their own, but at least they had
hope for the future.

 LATIN ROOTS

◼ Working with a partner, see how many English words you can think of which come from these Latin words:

scrībit (he writes)
spectat (he watches)
labōrant (they work).

Score one point for every correct answer.

◼ In each of the following sentences, a word is underlined. These words all come from Latin. Working with a partner, write down the Latin word that each English word comes from. Then write down what you think these words mean. You can find clues by looking carefully at the picture story *Pandora settles in*. For example:

The doctor wrote out a prescription.

Prescription: from the Latin word **scrībit** – a written message to a chemist.

1 The optimum time to do your homework is soon after school before you are too tired.

2 Nurses take care of invalids.

3 You can minimize the dangers of crossing the road by following the Green Cross Code.

4 What kind of job is a sedentary job?

5 This book is an introduction to Latin.

How did you do? Could you guess the meanings? Latin is useful for learning new English words!

Remember! Look at the end of a Latin verb to see **who** is doing the action. Latin doesn't need a word for "I" or "you" or "they". For example, rīdeō = **I** smile.

 WORDS TO REMEMBER

coquō I cook
faciō I do
intrō I enter
labōrō I work
legō I read

rīdeō I smile
scrībō I write
sedeō I sit
spectō I watch
semper always

subitō suddenly
ancilla slave girl
novus/nova new
nunc now

4 The best days of your life

A writing lesson

Roman children usually began school at about the age of seven. Children of rich families were often taught at home. Corinthus is teaching Flavia and Iulius.

1 Flāvia intrat. Iūlius intrat.

2 Flāvia et Iūlius sedent.

3 Corinthus docet.

4 Iūlius scrībit. Flāvia nōn scrībit.

5 Corinthus nōn laetus est.
Corinthus īrātus est.

6 Flāvia, cūr nōn scrībis?

fatīgāta sum.

WORDS TO HELP

docet teaches   **cūr?** why?
laetus happy   **fatīgāta** bored
īrātus angry

GRASP THE GRAMMAR

Remember! Action words are called **verbs**.
Naming words are called **nouns**.
Words used to describe nouns are called **adjectives**.

1 Pick out the **verbs** in the picture story. Can you remember what they mean? Look closely at the endings, to see if the person doing the action is "you", "he/she" or "they".

2 Corinthus is angry (**īrātus**). Flavia is bored (**fatīgāta**).
These words are **adjectives**, telling us more about the nouns they describe. Remember that in Latin, adjectives need to match their nouns (Flāvi**a**/fatīgāt**a**, Corinth**us**/īrāt**us**).

Here are pictures of some of the family with a short sentence describing each one. The adjectives are missing – choose one to fit each sentence. The adjective you choose must have the right ending as well as making sense! The first one has been done for you.

a Flavia doesn't do her writing, so Corinthus is (**īrātus/īrāta/callidus**).

The answer is **īrātus** (angry). Corinthus can't be **īrāta** because he is masculine.

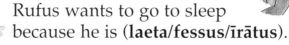
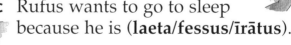

b Candidus sees Pandora, so he is (**īrātus/laetus/laeta**).

c Rufus wants to go to sleep because he is (**laeta/fessus/īrātus**).

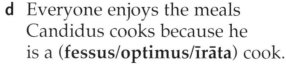

d Everyone enjoys the meals Candidus cooks because he is a (**fessus/optimus/īrāta**) cook.

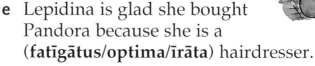

e Lepidina is glad she bought Pandora because she is a (**fatīgātus/optima/īrāta**) hairdresser.

ROMAN REPORT

Corinthus tries to make lessons more interesting for Flavia and Iulius by teaching them some Latin poetry. They are studying a long poem by the poet Virgil, which tells of the early history of Rome. First of all they read aloud lines of the poem. Then Corinthus tells them to copy out some lines. To write, Flavia and Iulius scratch on wax-covered tablets, using a special stick called a **stilus**. The **stilus** is pointed at the writing end but flat at the other end, so they can rub out mistakes. Sometimes they use a pen dipped in ink. The photo above shows Iulius's writing. Corinthus is not very pleased with it. If you look carefully, you can see the word **SEG**. which is short for **segniter**. This means "sloppy work"!

Flavia is obviously still bored. In the photograph on the left, you can see that she has smudged her work, and she has been doodling. She drew a horse and cart.

A Roman writer might practise with a **stilus** and wax tablet first, to make a draft. Then he would copy his work neatly with a pen. In Britain, people also wrote on very thin pieces of wood. Here are some Roman writing tablets and dip pens.

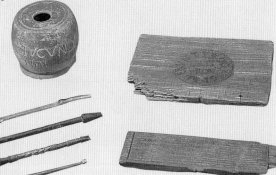

Rufus! Don't touch!

Rufus is too young for lessons, so he has been playing a game outside the room. Here is a gaming board and counters.

5 The ink goes flying.

6 Flavia is covered in ink. She tries to clean it off.

7 Corinthus tells her to put the mirror down and listen.

8 She keeps looking.

Corinthus decides to abandon the writing lesson and tells the children the story of someone who loved to look at his own reflection.

ECHO AND NARCISSUS

A beautiful girl called Echo once offended the goddess Juno. Juno punished Echo by making her repeat what other people said – she no longer had any words of her own. Echo fell in love with Narcissus. He was very handsome but vain and cruel. Echo followed him everywhere, repeating his words, but he wouldn't even look at her. She faded away with sorrow, until only her voice was left.

Narcissus made many other lovers unhappy, and so the gods decided to punish him too. One day, Narcissus saw his own reflection in a pool, and fell in love with it at once. He realized that he could never love anyone else as much, and stayed there, gazing into the water until he starved to death. In the place where he lay, the gods made a lovely flower grow – the narcissus. You can often find this flower growing beside a lake or pool, nodding for ever at its own reflection in the water.

LATIN ROOTS

▦ Can you think of any English words which come from **dormiō**?

▦ Would you be pleased if your teacher was in an <u>irate</u> mood?

(Use your dictionary to help you if you are stuck.)

> You have now met six different endings for a Latin verb. The endings change to show **who** is doing the action of the verb. This is how we usually write them out:
>
> labōr**ō** **I** work   labōrā**mus** **we** work
> labōrā**s** **you** work*   labōrā**tis** **you** work**
> labōra**t** **he/she** works labōra**nt** **they** work
>
> *one person ** more than one person

 WORDS TO REMEMBER

dormiō I sleep   **legō** I read
lacrimō I cry   **sedeō** I sit
labōrō I work   **rīdeō** I smile
scrībō I write   **cūr?** why?

Romans and Britons

Britons are best!

Rufus, Flavia and Candidus are kicking a ball. They sit down for a rest and begin to talk...

1. Rūfus et Flāvia et Candidus lūdunt.

2. Rūfus et Flāvia et Candidus sedent.

3. Flavia asks Candidus what life was like before he became a slave. Before the Romans conquered Britain, the British people lived in groups called *tribes*. Candidus belonged to the tribe called the **Brigantes**. Candidus daydreams about how his people used to live...

4. celeriter equitāmus...

5. ferōciter pugnāmus...

6. dīligenter colimus...

Who is doing the action when the verb ends in **-mus**?

WORDS TO HELP

celeriter quickly   **pugnō** I fight
equitō I ride   **dīligenter** carefully
ferōciter fiercely   **colō** I farm

GRASP THE GRAMMAR

In chapter 2, we learnt that we can make **nouns** more interesting by adding describing words, or **adjectives**, to them. In this chapter, we will see how to make **verbs** (action words) more interesting by using words which tell us **how the action is done**. We call these words **adverbs** (because they **add** to the **verb**).

Candidus said, "We ride *quickly.*" *Quickly* is an **adverb**.

1   Use an adverb to answer these questions, first in English and then in Latin.

   a How does Candidus describe the way that the Britons fight?

   b How does he describe the way that they farm the land?

Who has a good memory?
In chapter 4, Corinthus was not pleased with the way in which Iulius had copied out a piece of Latin. Corinthus used an **adverb** to describe how Iulius had worked. Can you remember it, in English or in Latin? (Look at page 23 if you are stuck!)

2   Look at the adverbs in English. Which two letters do you see at the end each time?

3   Look at the adverbs in Latin. Which three letters do you see at the end?

ROMAN REPORT

The Britons

Candidus is proud of the way his tribe could ride and fight and farm the land. When the Romans arrived in Britain they were surprised at how fast and skilful the British people were when driving their chariots. Julius Caesar, the first Roman commander to come to Britain (in 55 BC), described their warriors like this:

> They begin by driving all over the field hurling spears. The horses and the noise of the wheels make the enemy soldiers terrified. They train and practise every day and so they become so skilful that even on a steep slope they can control the horses at full gallop and stop them in a moment. They run along the chariot pole, stand on the yoke and get back into the chariot as quick as lightning.

What did the Romans think of the Britons and their country?

Although some British tribes fought hard against the Roman army, the Romans eventually defeated them and took control of England. This was because the Roman soldiers were professional and well organized.

One of the writing tablets from Vindolanda shows that some Romans thought they were better than the Britons: "The Britons are unprotected by armour. There are very many cavalry. The cavalry do not use swords, nor do the silly little Britons mount in order to throw javelins."

They didn't like us very much. They called us **Brittunculī** which means "silly little Britons".

Some Romans were obviously not impressed by what they heard about Britain either. For example, the writer Cicero said: "There is no hope for booty other than slaves, among whom you cannot expect any highly skilled in literature or music." However, another writer, Strabo, felt that there were certain things that the Romans could bring back from Britain: "Grain, cattle, gold, silver and iron are found in the island. They are exported together with animal skins, slaves and hunting dogs."

 LATIN ROOTS

The underlined words come from Latin words in the picture story *Britons are best!* Find the Latin word for each one to help you understand the meaning.

1 Would your teacher be pleased or angry with a <u>diligent</u> pupil?

2 Which English word comes from **ferōciter**?

3 A dog might be described as <u>pugnacious</u>. What does that mean?

4 What happens if you put your foot on the <u>accelerator</u> in a car? Which Latin word in the picture story has part of this word in it, and means something to do with speed?

Romans are best!

Flavia is trying to prove to Candidus that life is better now that the Romans rule Britain.

 WORDS TO HELP

tesserae mosaics
ita vērō yes
dīrēctae straight

commodae comfortable
nōbīscum with us

Is Candidus happy at Vindolanda?

Before the Romans came, Candidus's family farmed their own land. His father was brave and strong, and could fight in a chariot. On the other hand, Candidus and his family lived in a dark, smoky hut. The British tribes often fought each other and, when Candidus was a child, his village was destroyed by warriors from an enemy tribe. Candidus was taken prisoner and treated badly by his captors. He was glad when they sold him to a Roman family who were kind to him.

> Do you think that Candidus's life has improved now that he works for a Roman family? Does he agree with what Flavia and Rufus say? Explain why you think it is a better life – or not.

Rufus wants a story. Corinthus offers to tell him another Greek myth but Candidus interrupts. "No, it's my turn to tell Rufus a story. We have some great British tales of our own."

A TRAVELLER'S TALE

I heard this story as a child, by the fireside in our smoky hut. It was told by an old traveller from the West. As you know, Britain is a great island. The seas round it are filled with small islands, some inhabited by people but others only by ghosts. Roman ghosts belong under the earth, but the spirits of British heroes haunt the sacred islands. The traveller told us of a terrible experience he had when he was a young fisherman. He was rowing his boat in rocky coastal waters when a sudden storm blew up from a cloudless sky. Without warning the sky darkened and thunder roared. Violent winds rushed over the sea, tossing the light boat on the vast waves, and flinging it aground on a strange shore. Lightning flashes showed the fisherman that he was on an island. A single figure, in a long robe, stood on the shore. He was a Druid, a Celtic priest. The traveller fell on his knees in fear; he must be trespassing on a holy island.

"Somewhere, a great man has died," said the Druid. "The tempest you experienced was his spirit passing. Flee now, for you are in deadly danger as his spirit flies to this holy place in storm and fury."

The fisherman scrambled into his boat and rowed desperately away over a suddenly calm sea. When he reached land, he found that his hair had turned as white as bone from fear.

Remember that **adverbs** *describe* action words (**verbs**).

 WORDS TO REMEMBER

verbs	adverbs	nouns	phrases
lūdō I play	**celeriter** quickly	**viae** streets	**ita vērō** yes
equitō I ride	**ferōciter** fiercely	**vīllae** houses	**nōbīscum** with us
pugnō I fight	**dīligenter** carefully		

Let's go shopping!

Flavius and his family are planning to travel to the large town of Eboracum. Today, this town is called York. You can find it on the map of Roman Britain on page 1. Flavius and Lepidina have been to Eboracum before, when they first came to Britain from Holland, but this will be the children's first visit.

 WORDS TO HELP

vādō I am going
Eborācum to York
ibi there
arma weapons

lūdī games
pilulae beads
variae colourful

ROMAN REPORT

Travel

If you want to travel from Vindolanda to York today, you can go by car or by train, and the journey takes about two hours. In Roman times though, it was a much longer journey and it could be dangerous. Flavius and his family would have had an armed guard to protect them against bandits.

The distance between Vindolanda and York is 193km (120 miles). The family will travel in a covered wagon, and will only manage about 6km (4 miles) in one hour. How long will their journey take?

The family can't travel this far in a single day, so they will stop and rest at a **mānsiō** (inn) on the way to York, and again on their way home. The inns are at Cataractonium (today called Catterick) and at Vinovia (Binchester). The whole trip would probably have taken about a week.

Let's all go!

Candidus and Corinthus are going with the family, but Pandora is staying behind to look after Rufus. Corinthus wants to choose some new pens and wax tablets, and Candidus needs fish sauce and some new cooking equipment. He also hopes to see an old friend who lives in Eboracum.

1. vādō Eborācum. ibi stilī et cērae optimī sunt!

2. Barātes Eborācum habitat. Barātes amīcus est.

3. Rūfus lacrimat.

4. nōlī lacrimāre! venī Eborācum!
Rūfus rīdet.

5. Pandōra, venī Eborācum!
ita vērō!

6. Corinthus et Candidus rīdent.

 WORDS TO HELP

stilī pens
cērae wax tablets
habitat he lives

Eborācum in Eboracum *or* to Eboracum
amīcus friend

GRASP THE GRAMMAR

Now that the family is out of the way, it's time for me to check how you are getting on with Latin. Here's a mini-quiz. Choose the right answer – there's only one right answer each time.

1 An *action word* is called a noun/verb/adjective.

2 The *name* of a person, place or thing is called a noun/adverb/adjective.

3 A word that *describes* a person or thing is called a noun/verb/adjective.

4 In Latin, the *person* doing the verb is shown by the beginning/ending of the verb.

Here's some more practice on nouns and adjectives.

1 What do these sentences mean in English?

a stilus optimus est.
b stilī optimī sunt.
c tunica pulchra est.
d gladiī acūtī sunt.
e cēra frācta est.

f pilulae pulchrae sunt.
g Vibrissa obēsa est.
h Pandōra pulchra est.
i Corinthus callidus est.
j Candidus dūrus est.

WORDS TO HELP

stilus pen
gladius sword
acūtus/acūta sharp
cēra wax tablet

frāctus/frācta broken
obēsus/obēsa fat
dūrus/dūra tough

The family would not have made this journey to Eboracum very often. Imagine how they are feeling. How do you feel when you visit a big city? Describe how you think each person in the family is feeling.

A day in Eboracum

When the family arrives in Eboracum, the children are excited because it's such a big town. It is noisy and full of people. Everywhere, shopkeepers and traders are selling beautiful things from different parts of the Roman Empire. The whole family enjoys some shopping.

Here they are with the things they have bought – but the shopping is in a muddle! Can you sort it out?

pilulae glass beads	**stilī et cērae** pens and wax tablets	**lūdus** game board	**capillāmentum** wig
ampūlla perfume flask	**animālia aēnea** bronze animals	**gladius** sword	**mortārium** cooking pot

(All these items are in the Gardens Museum in York.)

For example: *Flavius buys a sword* (**gladius**).

LATIN ROOTS

The underlined words come from Latin words in this chapter. Find the right Latin word for each one to help you understand the meaning.

1 What is an animal's <u>habitat</u>?

2 If you were suffering from an <u>acute</u> stomach-ache, would it be a bad one?

3 What does an <u>obese</u> person look like?

4 If your arm is <u>fractured</u>, what's wrong with it?

ROMAN REPORT

Candidus meets his friend

In Eboracum, Candidus is very pleased to meet his old friend Barates. Barates is a trader, and on his stall he sells beautiful jewellery and rich cloth. He also makes flags for the Roman army. He and Candidus have a long talk. Barates explains that he left his home in Syria and followed the Roman army to Britain. He lived in London, where he met a slave girl, Regina, whom he loved and wanted to marry. He bought Regina's freedom, so that he could marry her. Then they moved up to the north, and now they are living in Eboracum.

The Roman Empire

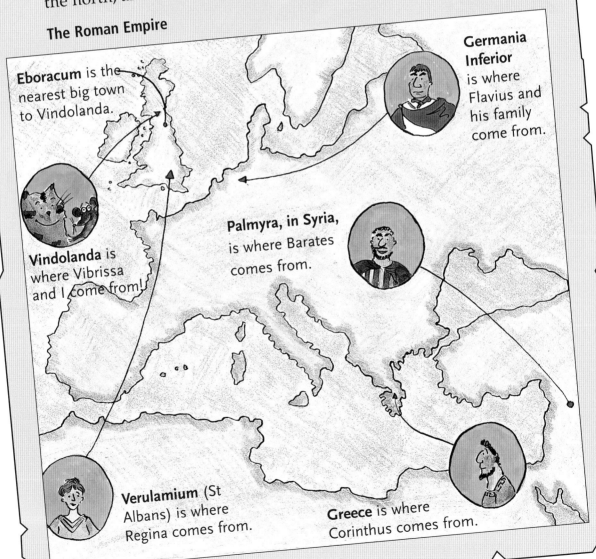

Eboracum is the nearest big town to Vindolanda.

Germania Inferior is where Flavius and his family come from.

Vindolanda is where Vibrissa and I come from!

Palmyra, in Syria, is where Barates comes from.

Verulamium (St Albans) is where Regina comes from.

Greece is where Corinthus comes from.

After a long day in Eboracum, Rufus is very tired and grumpy. Corinthus tells him a story.

ACTAEON AND DIANA

One day Actaeon was out hunting deer with his dogs. He happened to wander past the secret cave of the goddess Diana, and he saw her bathing. Diana couldn't reach her bow and arrows to shoot Actaeon, so the angry goddess threw water in his face. Immediately, antlers sprouted from Actaeon's forehead. His ears grew hairy and pointed, his neck stretched upwards, his arms grew long and thin and his hands hardened into hooves. Soon his whole body was covered in thick brown fur. When he saw his reflection in the bathing pool, he knew he had been turned into a stag.

Terrified, Actaeon fled into the forest, crashing through the brambles and leaping over fallen logs. He heard the familiar sound of hunting dogs on the scent. Actaeon's own dogs could not recognize their master, seeing only a fleeing stag. The well-trained animals chased Actaeon and tore him to pieces. This is how Diana punished Actaeon.

Remember what you have learned about **nouns** and **adjectives** in Latin. The adjective must always match the noun.

WORDS TO REMEMBER

arma weapons	**gladius** sword
lūdus game	**callidus/callida** clever
stilus pen	**habitat** he lives
cēra wax tablet	**ita vērō** yes

Be careful, Rufus!

Iulius and Rufus have been out to watch the soldiers practising with their weapons. Iulius wants to join the Roman army as soon as he is 18. He and Rufus return to the house, where Iulius asks Flavius about his weapons.

WORDS TO HELP

quid est? what is it?   **lōrīca** breastplate
galea helmet   **siste!** stop!
gladius sword   **pugiō** dagger
pīlum javelin   **relinque!** leave it!
scūtum shield   **perīculōsus** dangerous
cavē! be careful!   **ecce!** look!

 GRASP THE GRAMMAR

We are going to look at a different sort of verb. Remember that verbs are action words. In this picture story, Flavius tells Rufus to do things; he also tells him *not* to do things. For instance, he says **cavē!**, which means "Be careful!" and **siste!** (stop!) and **relinque!** (leave it!). Verbs like this are called **commands** or **orders**.

 We have already met some verbs like this. Can you remember them? Look at the clues in the brackets! Commands are easy to spot because they are followed by an exclamation mark!

venī! (Claudia wrote this to Lepidina.)

surge! (Lepidina said this to Vibrissa when she wanted her to chase Minimus.)

redī! (The whole family shouted this at Rufus when he knocked over the peacock.)

If you want to give a command to **more than one person** in Latin, you add **-te** to the end of the command. This is called the **plural form**.

 venī! = come!
(one person)

 venīte! (venī + te) = come!
(more than one person)

Simo dicit (Simon says)

This game will help you to remember the command words. Your teacher will give you some orders. If she says **Simō dīcit** followed by an order, you must do as she tells you. If she doesn't say **Simō dīcit** first, do nothing! Listen carefully, because she will try to catch you out! She will use the plural form of the Latin commands when she talks to the whole class.

Do as you're told!

Flavius and Iulius are watching the centurion. He is in charge of the soldiers and is giving them their orders.

WORDS TO HELP

mīlitēs soldiers
audīte! listen
sūmite! pick up
portāte! carry

prōcēdite! go forward
dēmittite! put down
testūdinem facite! make a tortoise

What is a "tortoise"?

The soldiers group closely together, and put their shields over their heads. It looks like a tortoise!

ROMAN REPORT

The centurion

The centurion looks different from the other soldiers. He wears a special helmet, and carries a stick. He wears medals on his chest, and shiny greaves (rather like shin-pads) to protect his legs. If the soldiers do not obey his commands, he uses his stick to punish them. When they are practising, the soldiers use weapons made of wood, which are not sharp.

LATIN ROOTS

Look back at the centurion's orders to help you with the meaning of the underlined words.

1 If you are doing <u>military</u> training, what are you?

2 What do you do in an <u>auditorium</u>?

3 What does a <u>porter</u> do?

4 You are having your passport checked at an airport. The officer checks it and then tells you to <u>proceed</u> to the plane. What does he mean?

5 What happens in a <u>factory</u>?

If you remember the Latin word, it will often help you to spell the English word correctly!

ROMAN REPORT

Off duty

The soldiers have finished training for the day and have some time to relax. Some of them are playing a board game, and they are betting with their pay. Iulius notices that one soldier seems to be winning all the time.

The soldiers are drinking a beer that was made near Vindolanda. When they run out, one of them writes a note to Flavius, asking him to order some more.

"The comrades have no beer. I ask that you order some more to be sent."

Iulius is very impressed by what he has seen. Later in the day, he talks to Corinthus and tells him about the bravery and skill of the soldiers. Corinthus agrees that Roman soldiers are strong and brave, but he reminds Iulius that you also have to be clever to win a war. He tells him how the famous Greek warrior, Odysseus, thought of a cunning way to get inside the walls of Troy.

ODYSSEUS'S CLEVER PLAN

The Greeks fought long and hard against the Trojans, but after ten years, they had still not managed to get inside the walled city of Troy to destroy it. Then Odysseus, the Greek warrior famous for his cunning, came up with a clever plan. The Greeks built a huge, hollow, wooden horse, and hid their best fighters inside it. They left the horse outside the gates of Troy. The Greeks then fooled the Trojans into thinking that they had left the battlefield and were sailing away, home to Greece. In fact, the Greek warriors were hiding on a nearby island. As night fell, the Trojans brought the enormous horse into their city. They believed it was a present for the goddess Minerva.

At dead of night, the Greeks opened a trapdoor and climbed down from the horse. They opened the gates of the city to their fellow Greeks, who quickly attacked the sleeping Trojans, killing many of them, and destroying the city.

Remember! Commands end in a vowel and are followed by an exclamation mark. When a command is given to more than one person, it ends in **-te**.

 WORDS TO REMEMBER

weapons
galea helmet
gladius sword
pīlum javelin
scūtum shield
pugiō dagger
lōrīca breastplate

commands
audīte! listen!
redīte! go back!
siste! stop!
prōcēdite! go forward!

8 Clean and healthy

Time for a bath!

In the morning, Lepidina and Flavia usually visit the military bath-house. Here they meet their women friends. They begin with some exercises.

1. Lepidīna et Flāvia hilariter lūdunt.

2. Lepidīna et Flāvia in apodytēriō sunt. celeriter exuunt.

3. Lepidīna et Flāvia in tepidāriō sunt. segniter recumbunt.

4. Lepidīna et Flāvia in caldāriō sunt. ancillae prūdenter rādunt.

5. Lepidīna et Flāvia in frīgidāriō sunt. breviter summergunt.

6. Lepidīna et Flāvia cum amīcīs garriunt. laetae et pūrae sunt.

WORDS TO HELP

hilariter cheerfully
lūdunt they are playing
in apodytēriō in the changing room
exuunt they are undressing
in tepidāriō in the warm room
segniter lazily
recumbunt they are lying down
in caldāriō in the hot room
ancillae slave girls

prūdenter skilfully
rādunt they are scraping their skin
in frīgidāriō in the cold room
breviter for a short time
summergunt they plunge underwater
cum amīcīs with friends
garriunt they are chatting
laetae happy
pūrae clean

 GRASP THE GRAMMAR

Remember that action words are called **verbs**, and words which tell us *how* the **verbs** are done are called **adverbs**. In Latin, the adverbs you have met end in **-ter**.

1 Here are five sentences in which people are doing things. Copy the sentences out, making each one more interesting by filling in the gap with an **adverb**. Choose from the list below. You can use each adverb only once. Then write down what the whole sentence means in English.

   a Vibrissa et Minimus _____ currunt.

   b Lepidīna et Flāvia _____ ambulant.

   c Pandōra et Corinthus _____ labōrant.

   d Rōmānī et Britannī _____ pugnant.

   e Lepidīna et Flāvia _____ summergunt.

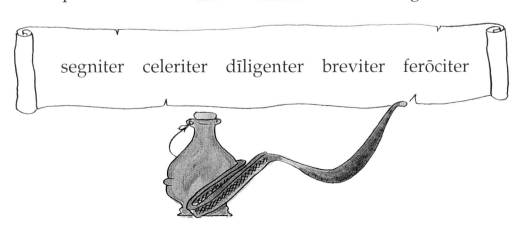

segniter   celeriter   dīligenter   breviter   ferōciter

ROMAN REPORT

The public baths

In Roman times, only rich people had water piped right into their houses. In most households, water had to be collected from tanks or fountains nearby, so most people managed with a quick wash in the morning. They would enjoy a much longer soak when they visited the public baths later in the day.

A visit to the baths would begin with some exercise to work up a sweat. The bathers would then undress and leave their clothes in the changing room (**apodytērium**). Next they went to the warm room (**tepidārium**) where they lay on benches. After relaxing and chatting for a while, they moved into the hot room (**caldārium**). They lay down again while their slaves, who accompanied them to the baths, rubbed oil onto their bodies. The oil would then be scraped off with a metal scraper called a **strigil**. Any dirt on the skin came off with the oil. The visit would finish with a cold plunge bath in the cold room (**frīgidārium**).

The bath-house at Vindolanda was built for the soldiers but other people living near the camp could use it too. Normally, men and women bathed separately – either in separate bath-houses (as in Pompeii) or at different times of the day.

Which room is which? They are all muddled up here! Can you match each Latin name with its English meaning?

1 tepidārium   a cold room
2 frīgidārium   b changing room
3 apodytērium   c hot room
4 caldārium   d warm room

- What cold object does **frīgidārium** remind you of?
- What temperature is <u>tepid</u> water?

MINIMUS VISITS THE BATHS

I followed Flavia and Lepidina to the baths this morning, and sneaked into all the rooms with them. Let me show you round!

You can exercise or meet your friends here.

The furnace is here. It burns all day, sending hot air flowing under the floors.

This is where you start to warm up.

This is the cold bath!

It's very hot in here! This is where you have your skin oiled and scraped to clean it.

This is where you take your clothes off, and put on wooden clogs – the floors get very hot!

This is the latrine. It has running water. The Romans have excellent hygiene!

A visit to the doctor

When Lepidina and Flavia get home, they find Flavius in a terrible mood. He has sore, red eyes. Lepidina takes him off to the doctor.

WORDS TO HELP

discumbe! lie down
oculōs aperī! open your eyes
impōne! put it on
trīs per diem three times a day

cōnsūme! eat
bis per diem twice a day
grātiās agimus thank you

The doctor at Vindolanda might have used some tools like these. The palettes and mixing tools were used to mix eye medicines like Flavius's ointment. The scalpels were used in operations. The doctor might have used the hooks for pulling out tonsils!

> If we see a doctor, he or she tells us what to do to get better. The doctor at Vindolanda did the same for Flavius. Can you find all the words the doctor says which are commands? Write them down in Latin, and then write down what they mean in English.
>
> Why do some of the commands end in **-te?**

Flavius is having trouble seeing because of his sore eyes. Rufus and the other children look closely at Flavius's eyes and are pleased when the ointment starts to work. Meanwhile, Candidus tells them a story about a giant with only one eye: the Cyclops.

ODYSSEUS AND THE CYCLOPS

On their way home from Troy, Odysseus and his fellow Greeks had many adventures. One of the most exciting was an encounter with a terrible giant, called a Cyclops, who had one huge eye in the middle of his forehead.

On their travels, the Greeks stumbled across the Cyclops's cave, full of fat sheep and baskets of cheese. They wanted to rush back to their ship but Odysseus was curious, and wanted to meet whoever lived in the cave. He had brought wine to exchange for food. When the monster arrived, the Greeks were terrified and wished they hadn't waited! The Cyclops ate three of the men, and then closed the cave mouth with a boulder. They were trapped! Then cunning Odysseus gave his strong wine to the Cyclops, making him drunk. The Cyclops collapsed on the floor, snoring. Odysseus picked up a big stick, sharpened the end and heated it in the fire, before plunging it deep into the Cyclops's single eye.

Although he was blind, the monster was determined not to let the men escape. He sat at the mouth of the cave and felt the backs of the sheep as they left for the pastures. So Odysseus tied his men under the sheep, and clung on tightly under the biggest ram himself. Odysseus and his men left the cave safely, and sailed away.

Adverbs describe verbs. They end in **-ter**. **Commands** come from verbs and are followed by an exclamation mark (!)

WORDS TO REMEMBER

apodytērium changing room
tepidārium warm room
caldārium hot room
frīgidārium cold room
breviter briefly
hilariter cheerfully
segniter lazily
prūdenter skilfully

Who's who?

Iulius has been asking his father more about the Roman army. Some of the soldiers wear special uniforms and he wants to know why.

 WORDS TO HELP

signifer standard-bearer
vēxillifer flag-bearer
cornicen horn-player
centuriō centurion

Who does what?

The **signifer** carries the standard (a sign or emblem) identifying his part of the legion. The standard is carried into battle in front of the soldiers. He is also in charge of the men's savings. The **vēxillifer** carries a flag made of brightly coloured silk. Perhaps his flag has been supplied by Barates (whom we met in chapter 6). The **cornicen**'s horn plays an important part in the fort's daily routine, signalling when duties begin and end as well as sounding alarms. The **centuriō** (whom we met in chapter 7) commands a troop of 80 men.

How soon can I join?

To a thirteen-year-old boy, a soldier's life sounds very exciting. Iulius wants to join the Roman army as soon as possible. He wants to travel and see the world, and he thinks it will be a great honour to belong to the Roman army. Flavius tells him that it is very unusual for a young man to join up before he is 18.

> How long will Iulius have to wait before he can join up?

Flavius also tells Iulius that he will have to have a medical check-up first, to make sure that he is fit. He can expect to be in the army for at least 20 years. He will be paid, but he will have to buy his food and some of his equipment out of his pay.

He will have to promise to be loyal to the Roman Emperor. He could be sent anywhere in the Roman Empire, and may have to be away from his home country for a long time. When he marches, he will wear his heavy armour and carry his own food, cooking pots and an axe for chopping wood. At the end of each day's marching, he will have to help set up the camp. He must always obey the orders of the centurion and will be severely punished if he is lazy or doesn't do what he is told.

> So that's why the centurion always carries a stick!

Imagine you are Iulius. Now that you have listened to Flavius, are you still so eager to join the Roman army? What would you like best about being in the army? What might be the problems?

Talk about this with a partner and then write two lists, showing the good and the bad points of a Roman soldier's life. See if you can find more information from books or other sources.

ROMAN REPORT

More socks please!

Most of the soldiers at Vindolanda came from the Netherlands, but some came from even further away, from hot countries. They must have found the winter weather at Vindolanda very cold. One soldier wrote home to ask for some more clothes. Here is the reply he received from his mother.

I have sent you some pairs of socks, two pairs of sandals and two pairs of underpants.

The ballista

Iulius and Flavius walk round the camp and see some soldiers practising with a **ballista**, a huge catapult that fires stone balls. The soldiers are using wooden balls for target practice. Iulius thinks the **ballista** must be a very frightening weapon when the soldiers use it in a real battle against the enemy. He asks the soldiers if he can try to fire it but he is not big enough to pull back the strong spring!

Where are Minimus and Vibrissa?

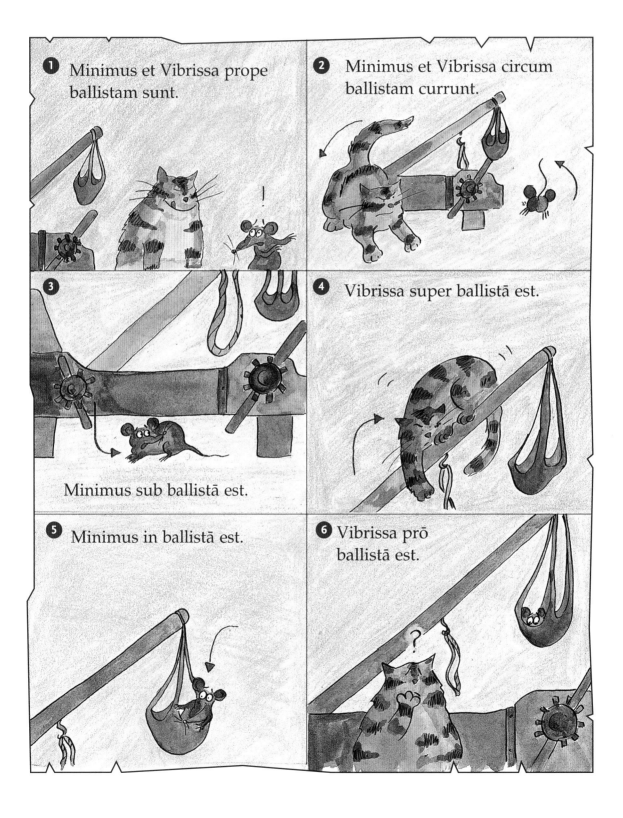

1 Minimus et Vibrissa prope ballistam sunt.

2 Minimus et Vibrissa circum ballistam currunt.

3 Minimus sub ballistā est.

4 Vibrissa super ballistā est.

5 Minimus in ballistā est.

6 Vibrissa prō ballistā est.

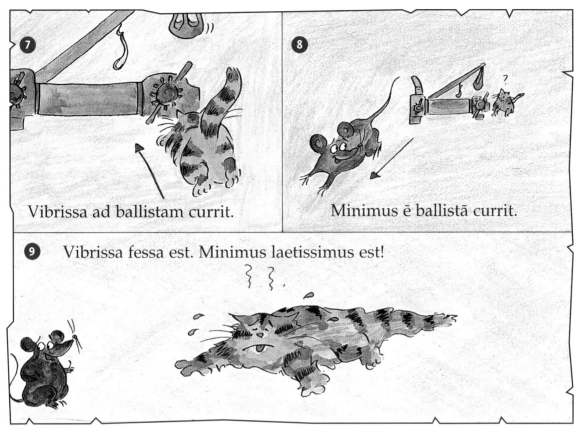

7 Vibrissa ad ballistam currit.

8 Minimus ē ballistā currit.

9 Vibrissa fessa est. Minimus laetissimus est!

 WORDS TO HELP

prope near	**super** on top of	**ad** to
circum round	**in** in	**ē** away from
sub under	**prō** in front of	**fessa** tired
		laetissimus very happy

 GRASP THE GRAMMAR

Have another look at the picture story and find the little words which tell you where Minimus and Vibrissa are. These words are called **prepositions** because they tell you the **position** of someone or something. In each of the first eight pictures, there is a **preposition**. Can you say which word it is in Latin, and then say what it means?

 LATIN ROOTS

1 Where does a <u>submarine</u> go?

2 **terra** is the Latin word for "earth", "ground", or "world". So where does a <u>subterranean</u> creature live?

3 If a yachtsman has <u>circumnavigated</u> the earth, where has he been?

4 In which direction does a <u>propeller</u> move a boat?

Iulius and Flavius have returned to the house. Iulius sees Corinthus and Candidus and complains, "I wish I could join the army now, but Father says I'm too young. I wish someone could stretch me to make me grow more quickly!" Candidus laughs: "But you can't stretch people!" "You've obviously never heard this story," replies Corinthus. "Let me tell you about..."

PROCRUSTES AND HIS TERRIBLE BED

You've probably heard of Theseus, the great Greek hero, and how he fought the Minotaur on the island of Crete. However, before he sailed to Crete, Theseus made a long journey to Athens, through rough country infested with bandits and thieves. He began his career as a hero by killing most of the wicked men he met on the way: the worst of these villains was Procrustes.

Procrustes kept a wayside inn, open to tired travellers. He would give his guests a friendly welcome and treat them well... until night-time. For when a weary traveller climbed into the bed Procrustes showed him, he was doomed. Procrustes would tie the unfortunate man to the bed and measure him. If he was longer than the bed, Procrustes cut his feet off. If he was shorter, Procrustes cranked a handle and turned the bed into a torturer's rack, stretching the victim until he died. If the traveller happened to be the right size for the bed, Procrustes simply suffocated him with a pillow. He then stole the traveller's money.

Theseus had heard of this evil man and was ready for him. When Procrustes showed him the famous bed, Theseus knocked him down, tied him to the bed, stretched him to twice his proper size and then cut off his feet and his head. That was the end of Procrustes!

 WORDS TO REMEMBER

quis? who?	**in** in/on
prope near	**prō** in front of
circum round	**ad** to
sub under	**ē** away from
super on top of	**fessus/fessa** tired

Remember! **Prepositions** tell us the position of something.

You look lovely

Pandora is helping Lepidina to dress. Lepidina is wearing a **tunica** (long dress). To keep Lepidina warm, Pandora also puts on her **palla** (shawl) and fastens it with a brooch.

WORDS TO HELP

grātiās tibi agō I thank you **unguentum** lip gloss
capillāmentum wig **gemmae** jewels
capillī hair **quamquam** although
aurēs ears **diū** for a long time

A Roman dressing table.

A child's sock.

GRASP THE GRAMMAR

In the picture story, the Latin sentences become longer when two short sentences are linked together by a joining word. For example:

Lepīdina laeta est **quod** Pandōra dīligenter labōrat.
Lepidina is happy *because* Pandora works skilfully.

quod (*because*) is the joining word.

We call these joining words **conjunctions**. Unlike adjectives and verbs, they never change their ending.

1 Have another look at pictures 2, 4, and 6. In each picture, what is the **conjunction** which links two short sentences together? Find the word in Latin and then say what it means in English.

2 Just as in Latin, we can make English sentences longer and more interesting by joining them together with **conjunctions**. Here are four pairs of English sentences. Join each pair to make one long sentence, using a **conjunction**. Choose from the list below. You can use each conjunction only once.

  a Pandora dresses Lepidina. She arranges her hair.
  b Pandora arranges Lepidina's hair carefully. She does not like it.
  c Corinthus and Candidus are happy. Pandora has arrived
  d Corinthus likes Pandora. Pandora likes Rufus.

because but and although

The romantic ring

WORDS TO HELP

in cubiculō in the bedroom
ānulus ring
pretiōsus valuable
cūr? why?
aureus made of gold

ā patre tuō from your father
haec verba these words
anima mea my life *or* my soul
amātōrius romantic

Look at the first picture of *The romantic ring*. Which Latin word is the **conjunction**? What does it mean in English?

LATIN ROOTS

1 Which English word, meaning valuable, comes from **pretiōsus**?

2 Which English word, meaning a gift, comes from the Latin word **dōnum**? (**Clue**: it is often used about money.)

3 What does it mean if we say that a person behaves or speaks in an <u>animated</u> way?

4 If you wrote a story and your teacher criticized it for being <u>verbose</u>, what would she mean?

If you find some of these words tricky, get help from a dictionary. Dictionaries are excellent books – they help me to learn new words!

Do you have any jewellery at home? What is it made of? Use a library to research the materials that the Romans used to make jewellery. What materials might they have had at Vindolanda? Are there materials used for jewellery today which would not have been available to the Romans?

Lepidina and Flavia are still admiring Lepidina's ring. Corinthus comes to tell Flavia that it is time for a lesson. She tells him that she loves the gold in her mother's ring and would like to have a gold ring too. Corinthus agrees that it is beautiful, but warns her about being greedy for gold.

MIDAS AND THE GOLDEN TOUCH

The god Bacchus was grateful to King Midas, and as a reward, granted him a wish. The greedy Midas wanted everything he touched to turn to gold. The god granted this wish, warning Midas that he would be sorry. Midas was thrilled. He touched a blade of grass with one cautious finger. Immediately it shone with a golden gleam. He picked a flower, and found it suddenly heavy in his hand, glittering. Midas hurried into his palace, touching everything he passed. Bright gold statues stood in his courtyard, between golden plants and pillars. Midas laughed. He bent to splash his fingers in the fountain, and the water suddenly stilled as the leaping streams became solid metal. He reached up to pick an apple but, before he could bite into it, found it hard and cold in his hand. He began to feel uneasy. Then he heard footsteps and a laughing voice, as his young daughter ran up to kiss him. Midas thoughtlessly held out his arms – and was horrified to feel his beloved daughter's warm skin go cold. His golden touch had turned her into a lifeless statue! Midas fell to his knees and prayed to Bacchus to undo his terrible gift. Bacchus forgave the greedy king, telling him to wash away the golden touch in the river Pactolus. The river still has a golden gleam to this day.

Remember the conjunctions (joining words) **et**, **sed**, **quod** and **quamquam**. Can you remember what they mean?

WORDS TO REMEMBER

grātiās tibi agō I thank you
laetus/laeta happy
diū for a long time
cūr? why?
quid? what?
ubi? where?

11 A sad day

Bad news

Candidus receives a letter from his friend Barates. Barates is very unhappy because his wife, Regina, has died.

1. Candidus epistulam accipit.

2. Barātes trīstissimus est quod Rēgīna mortua est.

3. Candidus tells Flavius and Lepidina the sad news. They decide to travel to Eboracum to attend Regina's funeral. Candidus will travel with Flavius and Lepidina to look after them on the journey. The other slaves will stay behind to take care of the rest of the family.

4. Lepidīna Candidum cūrat.

5. Corinthus equum et plaustrum parat.

6. Pandōra familiam cūrat.

WORDS TO HELP

epistulam letter
accipit receives
trīstissimus very sad
mortua dead

cūrat she looks after
equum horse
plaustrum cart
parat he prepares

GRASP THE GRAMMAR

The Latin word for a letter is **epistula**. Look back at the first picture of *Bad news* – it has a different ending, **epistulam**. Let's find out why.

> In chapter 2 you learnt that **adjectives** (describing words) have different endings because they must match the noun that they are describing.
>
> In chapter 3 you learnt that **verbs** have different endings, depending on who is doing the action.
>
> In this chapter, you will see that **nouns** also change their endings, **depending on the job they are doing in the sentence**.

Words can do different jobs in a sentence. The person or thing doing the action is called the **subject** of the sentence. The person or thing having the action done to them is called the **object** of the sentence.

> Remember that the **verb** is the action word in the sentence.

	subject	*verb*	*object*
For example:	Candidus	writes	a letter.

In Latin, nouns which are the object of a sentence change their endings. That's why **epistula** becomes **epistulam** – because it's the object of the sentence.

The Latin word for horse is **equus** but in picture 5 it becomes **equum**. This is because the horse is not the **subject** of the sentence (doing the action) but the **object** (having the action done to it – "being prepared").

1 Copy out these English sentences and underline the **verb**. Then put an **s** over the **subject** and an **o** over the **object**. The first one is done for you.

  s   o
a Vibrissa <u>chases</u> Minimus.

b Minimus chases Vibrissa.
c Minimus eats cheese.
d Vibrissa eats mice.
e Flavius and Lepidina praise Candidus.
f Candidus roasts a peacock and a dormouse.
g Candidus and Corinthus like Pandora.
h Pandora loves Rufus.

 LATIN ROOTS

1 Which English word, with a meaning similar to "receives", comes from the Latin word **accipit**?

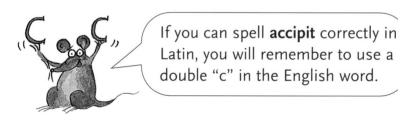

If you can spell **accipit** correctly in Latin, you will remember to use a double "c" in the English word.

2 In the Bible, what are the <u>epistles</u> of Saint Paul?

3 Check the meaning of the Latin word **mortua**. Now answer these questions, which all involve this Latin word. Use a dictionary if you get stuck.

a What is a <u>mortuary</u> used for?
b What does it mean to be <u>mortal</u>?
c What is special about an <u>immortal</u>?
  Whom did the Greeks and Romans believe to be immortal?

Goodbye to Regina

Candidus, Flavius and Lepidina arrive in Eboracum, where Barates is preparing for Regina's funeral.

1. Barātes corōnam portat.

2. Flāvius lucernam portat. Lepidīna ānulum portat.

3. sculptor titulum splendidum sculpit.

4. After Regina's body has been cremated, her bones are collected and put into a pot; the pot is then put into a pit with other items which Regina may need in the next world.

5. Flāvius et Lepidīna lucernam et ānulum in ōllam dēpōnunt.

6. Barātes corōnam in sepulcrum pōnit.

WORDS TO HELP

corōnam wreath
lucernam lamp
titulum inscription (*on a gravestone*)
sculpit he carves

ōllam pot
dēpōnunt they put down
sepulcrum tomb
pōnit places

Have another look at the Latin sentences in the picture story. In each one, find and write down the person who is doing the action (the **subject**), and the thing which is having the action done to it (the **object**). For example, the subject of the first sentence is **Barātes**, and the object is **corōnam**.

ROMAN REPORT

The Romans believed that it was very important to bury their dead correctly, following certain customs, to ensure that the spirit of the dead person could rest in peace in the next world.

In early Roman times, bodies were usually cremated; the ashes were then put into containers made of glass or lead. Later, burial became more common: the body, usually inside a coffin, was placed inside a burial mound. Things which the dead person might need in the next world, such as food and drink, would be placed in the container of ashes or in the coffin.

Sometimes a small coin was placed on the dead person's tongue. The Romans believed that, when they arrived in the Underworld, they had to cross the River Styx. They would be rowed across by Charon, the ferryman. The coin was to pay the fare.

Roman law did not allow burial in cities so the cemeteries are mostly to be found on main roads leading from Roman settlements.

Regina's tombstone tells us that she died aged 30. Why might she have died at such a young age?

Barates must have spent a lot of money on her tombstone. What does this tell us about Barates and Regina?

After the funeral, the family says goodbye to Barates. They travel to Cataractonium where they spend the night in the **mānsiō**. They feel tired and sad, but are pleased that they could be with Barates. They talk about death. Flavius tells Candidus the famous story of two lovers who died tragically – Pyramus and Thisbe.

PYRAMUS AND THISBE

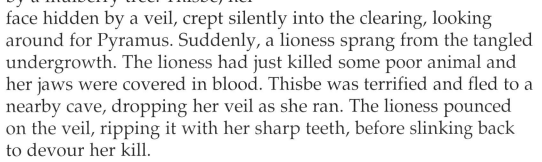

Pyramus and Thisbe were very much in love but they were forbidden to meet because their families were enemies. They arranged to meet each other secretly one night, in a clearing, by a mulberry tree. Thisbe, her face hidden by a veil, crept silently into the clearing, looking around for Pyramus. Suddenly, a lioness sprang from the tangled undergrowth. The lioness had just killed some poor animal and her jaws were covered in blood. Thisbe was terrified and fled to a nearby cave, dropping her veil as she ran. The lioness pounced on the veil, ripping it with her sharp teeth, before slinking back to devour her kill.

Pyramus arrived in the now deserted clearing. Seeing the blood-stained veil, and no sign of his beloved Thisbe, he assumed that she had been killed by the lioness. Desperate, and feeling that he could not live without her, Pyramus stabbed himself with his own sword. Soon afterwards, Thisbe returned to the clearing and, to her horror, found Pyramus, who was now almost dead. Distraught, she snatched up his sword and killed herself. The lovers' blood stained the ground and soaked into the roots of the mulberry tree under whose spreading branches they had hoped to meet. This is why mulberries are a deep blood-red colour.

Remember that the person who does the action is called the **subject** of the sentence.

The person or thing affected by the verb is called the **object** of the sentence.

Latin **nouns** change their endings to show whether they are the **subject** or the **object** of a sentence.

 WORDS TO REMEMBER

accipit receives **pōnit** places
parat prepares **epistula** letter
portat carries **mortuus/mortua** dead

Regina's tombstone.

12 Gods! Hear our prayers!

Rufus is ill

Lepidina and Flavius are anxious because Rufus is ill. He has a high temperature and is complaining of pains in his stomach.

1. Rūfus nihil cōnsūmit quod calidus est.

2. Lepidīna anxia est et medicum arcessit.

3. Corinthus et Candidus nōn labōrant quod sollicitī sunt.

4. quamquam Flāvia et Iūlius pavidī sunt, in hortō lūdunt.

5. Minimus et Vibrissa trīstēs sunt et nōn currunt.

6. Flāvius anxius est sed epistulam scrībit.

WORDS TO HELP

nihil nothing
cōnsūmit he eats
calidus hot
arcessit she summons

sollicitī worried
pavidī frightened
trīstēs sad

Be careful – **calidus** with one "l" is a different word from **callidus** with two!

Can you remember what **callidus** means?

GRAMMAR REVISION

1 a Each Latin sentence in the picture story contains an **adjective** (a describing word) which tells us something about the person or the people in the picture. Write down the six **adjectives** in Latin, one from each sentence. Then write the English meaning beside them. For example: **1 calidus** = hot.

 b Three of the **adjectives** are **singular** and three are **plural**. Can you sort out which is which?

Lepidina is **anxia** but Flavius is **anxius**. Why do adjectives change their endings? And why would they be even more worried if Rufus were **calidissimus**?

2 a In each picture, two short sentences are made into one longer sentence by the use of a **conjunction** (a joining word). Write down the **conjunctions** in Latin along with their English meaning.

 b Can you remember any other **conjunctions** in Latin or in English? Make a list.

3 Look at the verbs in the picture story, for example:
Rūfus nihil **cōnsūmit**.
Corinthus et Candidus nōn **labōrant**.

Why do some of the verbs end in **-t** and some in **-nt**?

The doctor has not been able to help Rufus. Flavius and Lepidina decide to make a sacrifice and pray to the gods. Meanwhile, Candidus prays to the local British goddesses.

> Iuppiter! precēs nostrās audī! vīnum accipe!

> deae mātrēs! precem meam audīte!

WORDS TO HELP

precēs nostrās our prayers
vīnum wine

deae mātrēs mother goddesses
precem meam my prayer

4 When a **verb** is followed by an exclamation mark, it is in the **command** form. In the prayers, **audī!** and **audīte!** both mean "listen!". Why does Candidus's command have the **-te** ending?

ROMAN REPORT

The gods

Corinthus asks Candidus about the **deae mātrēs**. Candidus explains that they are goddesses of healing. Corinthus suggests that they pray to one of the Greek gods, but Candidus does not know their names. Corinthus tells him the names of the most important Greek gods, and explains that the Romans worship the same gods, but usually with different names.

Greek name	Roman name	Greek name	Roman name
Zeus	Jupiter	Ares	Mars
Hera	Juno	Athena	Minerva
Artemis	Diana	Hephaestus	Vulcan
Apollo	Apollo	Demeter	Ceres
Poseidon	Neptune	Hades	Pluto
Hermes	Mercury	Dionysus	Bacchus
Aphrodite	Venus		

5 Each member of the family is trying to help Rufus to get better. Here are two lists – a list of characters and a list of their actions. Write down the name of each character and, in Latin, what you think he or she is most likely to do to make Rufus feel better. Write out each full sentence in Latin and then translate it.

	characters	actions
a	Lepidīna	fābulam nārrat.
b	Flāvius	Rūfum lambit.
c	Iūlius	capillōs pectit.
d	Flāvia	cāseum dat.
e	Candidus	medicāmentum portat.
f	Corinthus	versum recitat.
g	Pandōra	plaustrum facit.
h	medicus	sacrificium facit.
i	Minimus	suāviter cantat.
j	Vibrissa	Rūfum tenet.

WORDS TO HELP

fābulam story   **cāseum** cheese   **sacrificium** sacrifice
nārrat tells   **dat** gives   **suāviter** sweetly
lambit licks   **plaustrum** cart   **cantat** sings
capillōs hair   **facit** makes   **tenet** cuddles
pectit combs

All's well that ends well...

1. nunc Rūfus nōn calidus est.
2. subitō Rūfus surgit.
3. nunc Rūfus rīdet.
4. omnēs rīdent.

WORDS TO HELP

nunc now
surgit gets up
omnēs everyone

Rufus enjoyed the story Corinthus told him while he was ill. He asks to hear it again. So Corinthus explains how Mercury came to be the messenger of the gods…

THE AMAZING BABY

One morning, Apollo the Sun God drove his flaming chariot across the sky. He looked down at the Earth below, at the fields and woods of Greece. There, in a meadow, he kept a herd of splendid white cows. Every morning, he would count them proudly. But this morning, his forehead creased in a frown. Six of his cows were missing... Apollo set out to search for them. There was no sign of them, not even hoofprints. Finally, he came to a cave on a lonely mountainside, where a beautiful woman sat spinning. Apollo asked to search the cave. "No!" she replied. "My baby is asleep in there, in his tortoise-shell cradle. He is only a day old. How would he know anything about your cows?" Just then, a strange sound floated out of the cave. Someone was playing music. Apollo peered inside. The baby sat on the floor, holding the tortoise shell. He had strung it with cow-gut and made it into a musical instrument. Apollo snatched the baby up. "Where are my cows?" he demanded. The baby smiled innocently, but Apollo insisted on taking him to Jupiter on Mount Olympus. "This baby has stolen my cows!" he shouted. Jupiter looked sternly down at the baby. "How did you manage it?" he asked. "I slipped out of the cave while my mother was asleep, and I tied bark over the cows' hooves so they wouldn't make tracks," answered the baby. "I'm sorry about your cows, Apollo. I'm too young to know right from wrong. Take this musical instrument in exchange." Jupiter laughed. "I think you are going to be the greatest trickster ever! Why don't you stay here, where I can keep an eye on you? I have just the job for you!" So Mercury, the youngest of the gods, became the gods' messenger, as well as the god of thieves and tricksters.

valēte!